Mr. Shipman's
Kindergarten Chronicles:

The First Day of School
Learning Workbook

by

Prudence Williams

Table of Contents

Trace
the
Alphabet

Trace each letter of the alphabet and practice saying each letter.

Standard -- CCSS.ELA-Literacy.L.K.1.a -- Print many upper and lowercase letters.

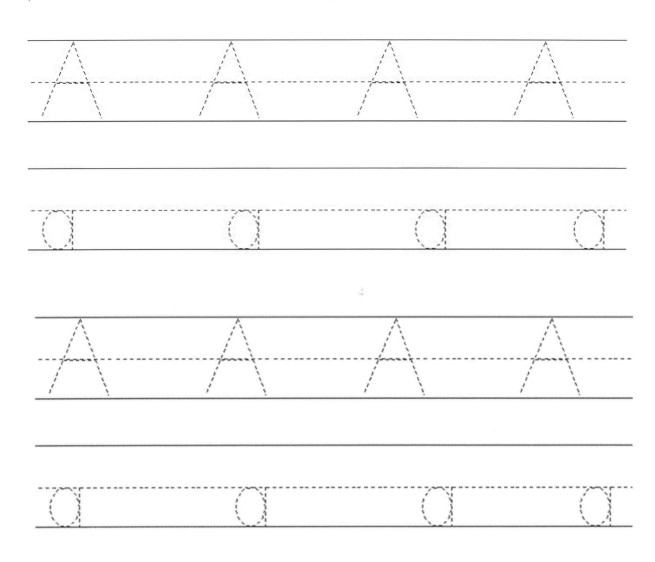

<u>A</u> is for <u>A</u>lyesi<u>a</u>.

<u>A</u>lyesi<u>a</u> is in Mr. Shipm<u>a</u>n's cl<u>a</u>ss.

ALYESIA

B B B B B

b b b b b

B B B B B

<u>B</u> is for <u>B</u>anicia.

<u>B</u>anicia is Dewayne's <u>b</u>ig sister.

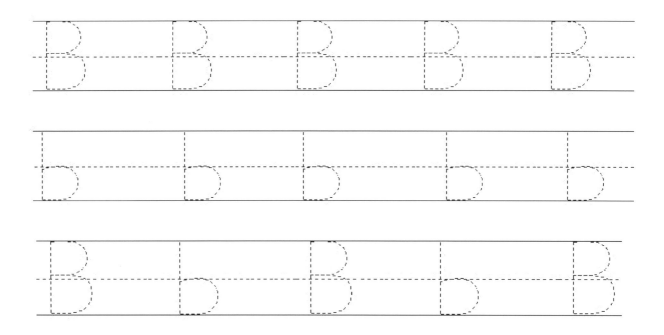

BANICIA

B B B B

b b b b b

B B B B B

C is for Clifford. Clifford goes to school.

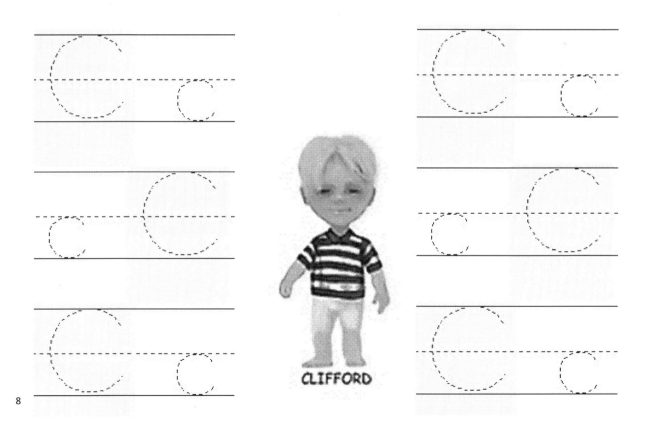

CLIFFORD

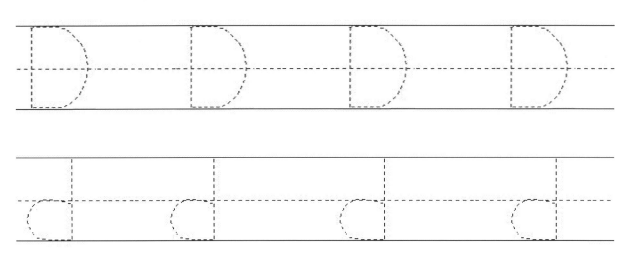

D is for **D**ewayne.

Dewayne likes to **d**raw in Mr. Shipman's class.

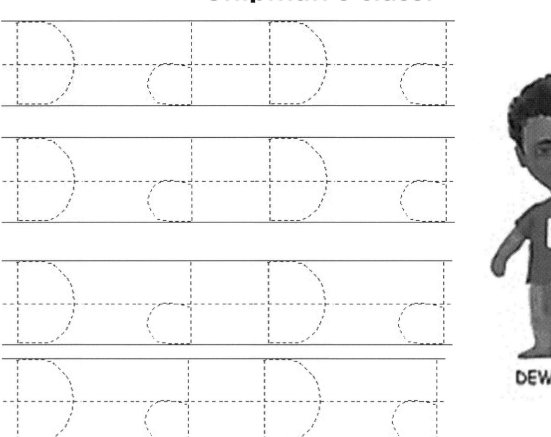

DEWAYNE

E is for <u>e</u>x<u>e</u>rcis<u>e</u>!
The kids and
Mr. Shipman
<u>e</u>x<u>e</u>rcis<u>e</u>.

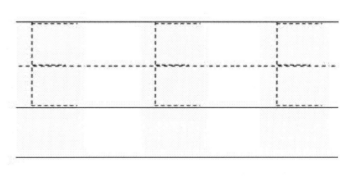

F is for flag!

Team Shipman has a flag!

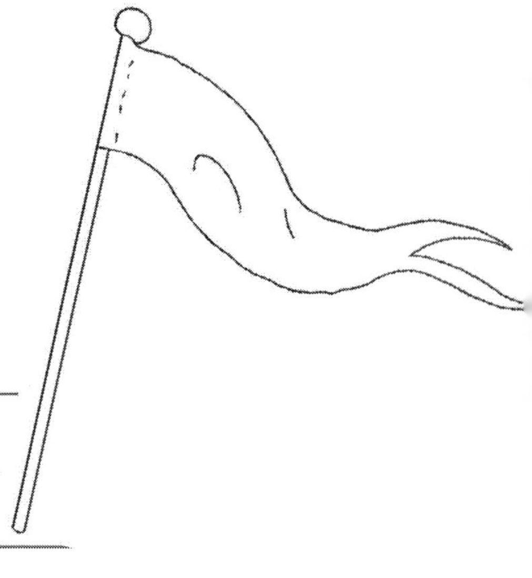

G is for great!

Mr. Shipman is a great teacher!

H is for **h**ugs. Clifford and **h**is mom **h**ug and say goodbye.

**I is for ice cream.
Tiffany loves ice
cream!**

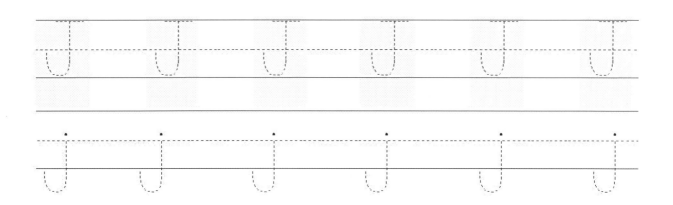

JAMARCUS

J is for **J**amarcus

Jamarcus **j**umps on his skateboard.

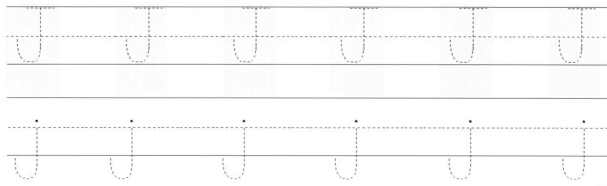

15

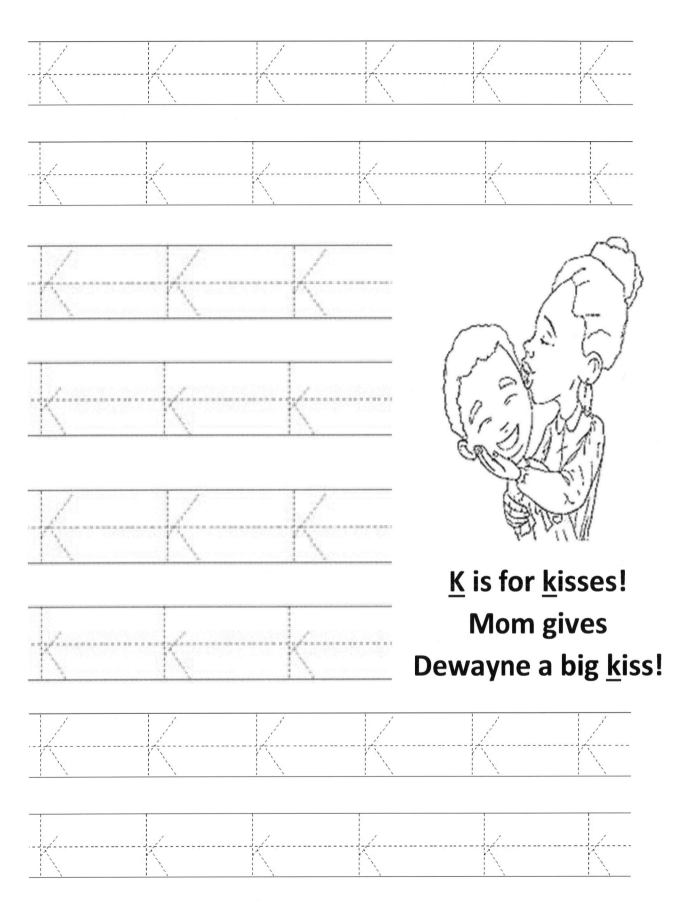

<u>K</u> is for <u>k</u>isses!
Mom gives
Dewayne a big <u>k</u>iss!

L is for **l**ift.

The boys **l**ift the dumbbe**ll**.

M is for **Mom!**

Dewayne loves his Mom!

N N N N N N

n n n n n n

N N N N N N

n n n n n n

N is for **N**ovember.

I**n** **N**ovember we celebrate Tha**n**ksgivi**n**g.

N N N N N N

n n n n n n

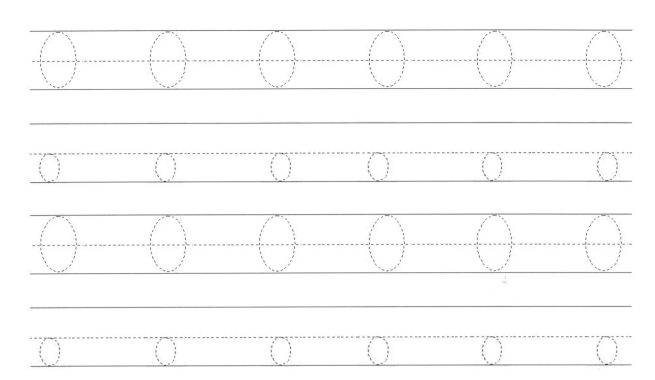

<u>O</u> is f<u>o</u>r <u>o</u>ut.

Mr. Shipman calls a time <u>o</u>ut, and Cliff<u>o</u>rd d<u>o</u>es n<u>o</u>t like it!

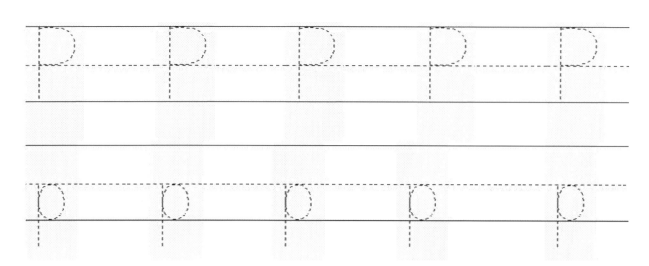

<u>P</u> is for <u>p</u>lay!

William p<u>l</u>ays

with the ball!

Q is for questions. Dewayne asks questions in Mr. Shipman's class!

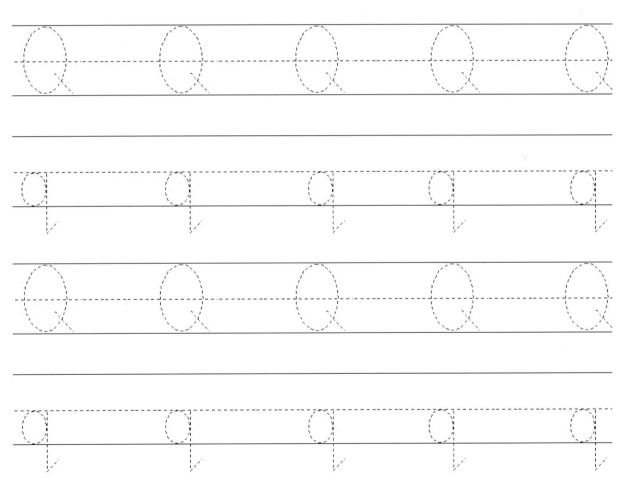

R R R R

r r r r

R is for <u>r</u>eindee<u>r</u>.

We made pape<u>r</u>

<u>r</u>eindee<u>r</u> in

M<u>r</u>. Shipman's class.

R R R R

r r r r

R R R R

r r r r

SUMMER

S is for Summer. Summer is a student in Mr. Shipman's class.

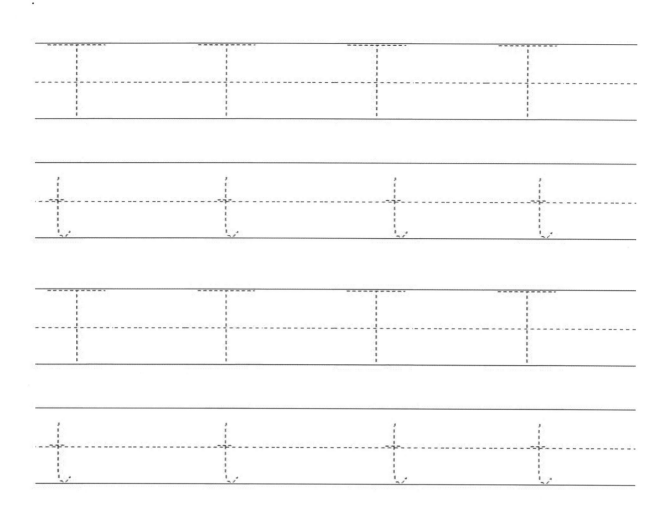

T is for **tee**t**er-**
tot**ter!**

The kids play
on
the teet**er-**
tot**ter!**

U is for
umbrella.

**Autumn
stays dry
under the
umbrella!**

V is for **v**iolin.

You might learn to play a violin in Mr. Shipman's class.

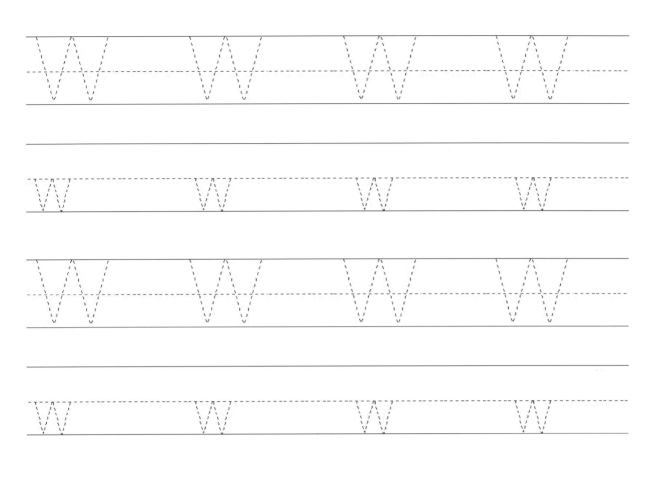

WILLIAM

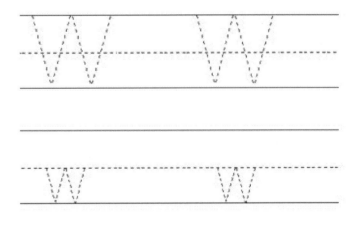

<u>W</u> is for <u>W</u>illiam.

<u>W</u>illiam runs <u>w</u>ith the kite.

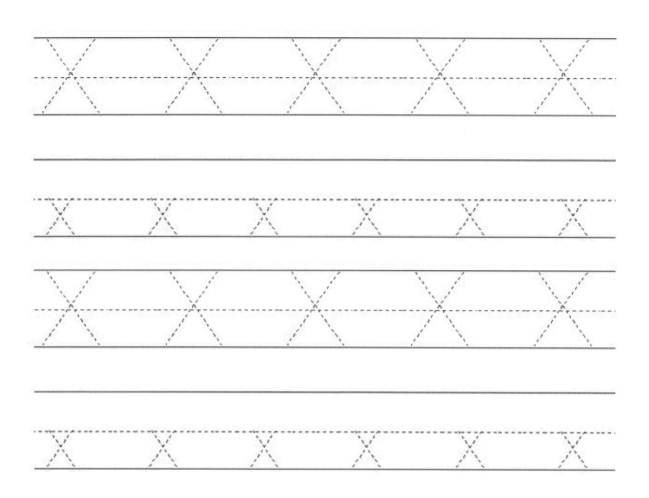

The letter X is in e_xcellent. Tiffany writes an e_xcellent 'X' on the board.

29

Y is for
yo**y**o! A
yo**y**o is
a great
to**y**!

Z is the last letter in the alphabet!

Dewayne practices writing the letter z.

Sight Words

Parents, sight words are words that are commonly used in language and reading. Students should recognize sight words without using phonetic interpretation. Create flash cards of the following lists of sight words and have your student practice reading and writing them. Work on one list at a time, studying words until students recognize each word at sight.

Standard -- CCSS.ELA-Literacy.L.K.1.b -- Use frequently occurring nouns and verbs.

List 1

1. I
2. Me
3. You
4. With
5. Hand
6. Leg
7. Head
8. Foot
9. Up
10. Down

List 3

1. Above
2. Fewer
3. Less
4. Paper
5. More
6. Hot
7. Cold
8. Bus
9. Car
10. Teacher

List 2

1. Walk
2. In
3. Out
4. Yes
5. No
6. Left
7. Right
8. Inside
9. Outside
10. Below

List 4

1. School
2. Friend
3. Book
4. Letter
5. Read
6. Can
7. The
8. Math
9. Number
10. Said

33

List 5

1. Music
2. Home
3. Quiet
4. See
5. Light
6. Water
7. Love
8. Like
9. Free
10. They

List 6

1. Play
2. Sun
3. Moon
4. go
5. Top
6. First
7. toys
8. Tree
9. Zoo
10. Cow

List 7

1. Pig
2. Tiger
3. Lion
4. Write
5. Fast
6. Snake
7. Bird
8. Mouse
9. Add
10. Fish

List 8

1. Cat
2. Dog
3. Pets
4. Yellow
5. Orange
6. Blue
7. Red
8. Black
9. Brown
10. Green

List 9

1. Colors
2. House
3. Clean
4. White
5. Have
6. Snack
7. Grandpa
8. Grandma
9. Baby
10. Wash

List 11

1. Ear
2. Queen
3. Under
4. Vase
5. Soon
6. Ride
7. Saw
8. Say
9. She
10. Very

List 10

1. Mom
2. Mother
3. Father
4. Dad
5. Sister
6. Brother
7. Where
8. Tray
9. X-ray
10. Want

List 12

1. That
2. Too
3. Well
4. Will
5. Year
6. An
7. It
8. Him
9. Her
10. For

List 13

1. Food
2. Of
3. Was
4. On
5. Off
6. At
7. From
8. How
9. About
10. Each

List 14

1. Do
2. Many
3. Some
4. These
5. Would
6. Into
7. Other
8. Two
9. One
10. All

List 15

1. Just
2. Words
3. Little
4. Big
5. Long
6. Water
7. May
8. Find
9. Only
10. Did

List 16

1. Quit
2. Now
3. made
4. People
5. Mad
6. Sad
7. Had
8. Them
9. Then
10. We

Tracing Sight Words

Practice tracing and reading each sight word.

Standards --

CCSS.ELA-Literacy.L.K.1.a -- Print many upper and lowercase letters.

CCSS.ELA-Literacy.L.K.1.b -- Use frequently occurring nouns and verbs.

Sight Words – Sight words are words that students identify by sight, not by phonetics.

Instructions – Trace each sight word and practice reading them.

Sight Words – Sight words are words that students identify by sight, not by phonetics.

Instructions – Trace each sight word and practice reading them.

Sight Words – Sight words are words that students identify by sight, not by phonetics.

Instructions – Trace each sight word and practice reading them.

Sight Words – Sight words are words that students identify by sight, not by phonetics.

Instructions – Trace each sight word and practice reading them.

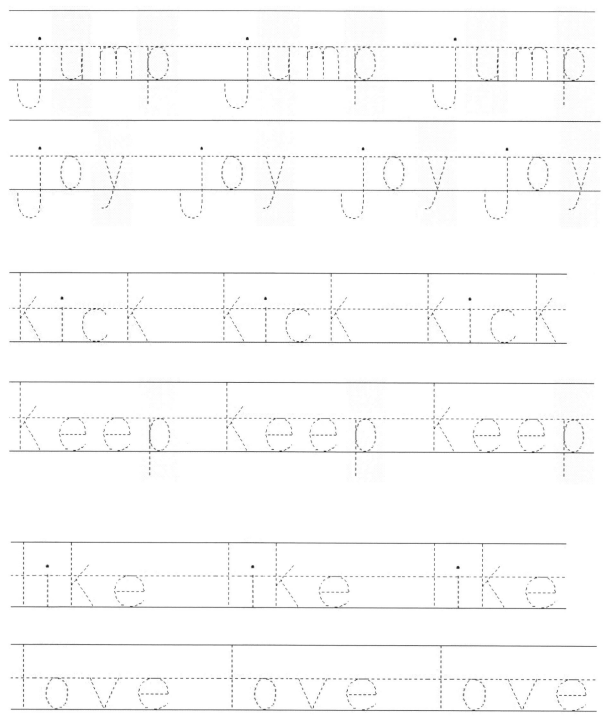

Sight Words – Sight words are words that students identify by sight, not by phonetics.

Instructions – Trace each sight word and practice reading them.

Sight Words – Sight words are words that students identify by sight, not by phonetics.

Instructions – Trace each sight word and practice reading them.

put put put put put

people people people

quit quit quit quit

quiet quiet quiet

read read read

red red red red

Sight Words – Sight words are words that students identify by sight, not by phonetics.

Instructions – Trace each sight word and practice reading them.

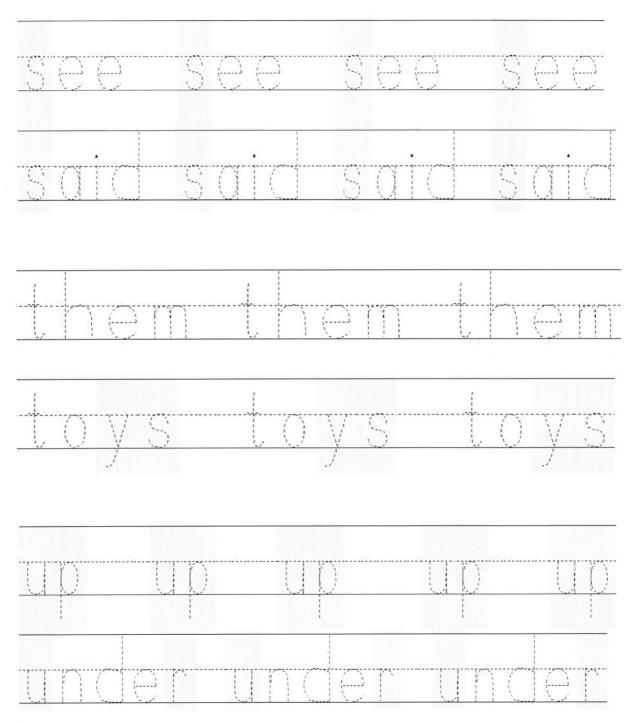

Sight Words – Sight words are words that students identify by sight, not by phonetics.

Instructions – Trace each sight word and practice reading them.

vase   vase   vase

very   very   very

was   was   was   was

we   we   we   we   we

xray   xray   xray   xray

you   you   you   you   you

yes   yes   yes   yes   yes

zoo   zoo   zoo   zoo   zoo

Nouns

Standard -- CCSS.ELA-Literacy.L.K.1.c -- Form regular plural nouns orally by adding /s/ or /es/ (e.g., dog, dogs; wish, wishes).

A **<u>noun</u>** is a word that represents a person, place, or thing.

Examples of nouns:

- A **<u>library</u>** is a place.

    _____

    -

    _____

        Write the word **library** above.

- A **<u>ship</u>** is a thing.

    _____

    -

    _____

        Write the word **ship** above.

- A **<u>Mr. Shipman</u>** is a person.

    _____

    -

    _____

        Write the word **Mr. Shipman** above.

A **noun** is a word that represents a place, thing, or person.

Circle the words that are nouns.

Dog	Run	Brother
Sister	School	Sit
Sing	Jump	Home
Read	Write	Cow
Cat	Rocket	Mother

Pick 6 nouns from above to write in the space provided below.

_____   _____
- - - - - - - - - - - - - - - - - -   - - - - - - - - - - - - - - - - - -
_____   _____

_____   _____
- - - - - - - - - - - - - - - - - -   - - - - - - - - - - - - - - - - - -
_____   _____

_____   _____
- - - - - - - - - - - - - - - - - -   - - - - - - - - - - - - - - - - - -
_____   _____

A **noun** is a word that represents a place, thing, or person.

Read each list of words below and select the noun from each list. Write the noun in the space provided.

List One:　　　Sing　　　Want　　　Leg　　　Jump

_____

- -

_____

List Two:　　　Table　　　Read　　　Write　　　Run

_____

- -

_____

List Three:　　　Wash　　　Mud　　　Clean　　　See

_____

- -

_____

List Four:　　　Kick　　　Swim　　　Smell　　　Tiger

_____

- -

_____

A **noun** is a word that represents a place, thing, or person.
Read the sentences below and underline all the noun(s) in each sentence.

1. The dog is black.

2. The boy is tall and smart.

3. The cat ran away.

4. The bird sings.

5. The mother hugged the little girl.

6. Whales live in the ocean.

7. Fish live in the pond.

8. Mr. Shipman is the teacher.

9. Dewayne learns to read.

10. The house is big.

Complete each sentence using a noun from the word bank below.

animals   books   houses   colors

1. Dogs and cat are _____.

2. Red and green are _____.

3. We read _____.

4. People live in _____.

A **<u>noun</u>** is a word that represents a place, thing, or person.

- When there is only one of a noun, it is **<u>singular</u>**.
- When there are more than one of a noun, it is **<u>plural</u>**.

Singular	Plural
Dog	Dogs
Mother	Mothers
Home	Homes
Rocket	Rockets
Fish	Fishes
Rose	Roses
Dish	Dishes
Bike	Bikes
Car	Cars
Hand	Hands
Cat	Cats

Circle the words that are plural from the list below.

Car	Homes	Rockets
Roses	Fish	Bike
Dishes	Mother	Hands
Dog	Rose	Cat

A **noun** is a word that represents a place, thing, or person.

- When there is only one of a noun, it is **singular**.
- When there are more than one of a noun, it is **plural**.

Read the sentences below. If the noun in the sentence is singular, (circle) it. If the noun in the sentence is plural, underline it.

1. The dogs are running.

2. The cat is yellow.

3. The houses are big.

4. Mom is sleeping.

5. Mr. Shipman is tall.

6. The school is open.

7. Girls are pretty.

8. The boy sat down.

9. The store is closed.

10. The baby is little.

Common Prepositions

Standard -- CCSS.ELA-Literacy.L.K.1.e
Use the most frequently occurring prepositions (e.g., to, from, in, out, on, off, for, of, by, with).

54

Common Prepositions

- In a sentence, there are words that let you know more information about the nouns and the verbs in the sentence. Many of these words are prepositions.
- Prepositions often tell us:
    o where a noun is
    o what is happening to a noun
    o when something is happening to a noun.

Common Prepositions

to	from	in	out	on
off	for	of	by	with

Examples of prepositions in sentences:

- Mr. Shipman went <u>to</u> his desk.

- Shuree came <u>in</u> the classroom <u>with</u> Banicia.

- Clifford took the ball <u>from</u> the toy box.

- Dewayne took his pencils <u>out</u> his bag.

- Mrs. Andrew held the door open <u>for</u> the students.

- Tiffany wrote <u>on</u> the paper.

- David took the box <u>off</u> the table.

- Jamarcus used a bottle <u>of</u> glue to finish the puppet.

- Maesa sat <u>by</u> Cameron.

- Hayden played <u>with</u> Sarafina.

Common Prepositions Activity -- Read the sentences below and circle the prepositions that best completes each sentence.

1. Mr. Shipman walked the class (**to** or **with**) the lunchroom.

2. Banicia ran (**out** or **off**) the door to meet her mom.

3. Shuree walked (**out** or **with**) her dad to Mr. Shipman's room.

4. The pirate ship hung (**from** or **for**) the ceiling.

5. Jamarcus sat (**by** or **off**) Clifford during circle time.

6. Autumn drew brown pictures (**of** or **on**) the paper.

7. Alyesia sat (**in** or **of**) a chair and waited for Mr. Shipman to talk.

8. Tatiana took her jacket (**off** or **on**) and sat down.

9. Leondra liked the picture Cameron drew (**of** or **on**) the brown doughnut.

10. Joseph and Sarafina opened the door (**for** or **off**) Ms. Andrews.

Now you complete the following sentences using one of the common prepositions to fill in the blanks.

11. Mr. Shipman talked _____the class each morning.

12. Banicia helped Dewayne put his school supplies _____ his bookbag.

Forming Sentences

Standards -- CCSS.ELA-Literacy.L.K.1.f -- Produce and expand complete sentences in shared language activities

CCSS.ELA-Literacy.L.K.1 -- Demonstrate command of the conventions of standard English grammar and usage when writing or speaking.

Form a sentence using the words on the board.

Write the sentence on the line below.

Remember, sentences start with capital letters and end with a period.

_____

_____

Form a sentence using the words in the bubbles. Write the sentence on the line below.

Remember, sentences start with capital letters and end with a period.

_____

_____

On the lines below, use the words given in the box to write three sentences about the picture above. Remember, a sentence starts with a capital letter and ends with a period.

1. They	7. Up	13. Her
2. She	8. Brother	14. Him
3. Clean	9. Sister	15. He
4. See	10. Read	16. Gives
5. Home	11. On	17. Sad
6. Paper	12. Hand	18. is

Sentence 1: _____

Sentence 2: _____

Sentence 3: _____

Question Words

Standard -- CCSS.ELA-Literacy.L.K.1.d -- Understand and use question words (interrogatives) (e.g., who, what, where, when, why, how).

Question Words

- When you do not know something, you ask a question.
- There are words that lets you know that a question is being asked.
- Some of these words are:

  - Who
  - What
  - When
  - Where
  - Why
  - How

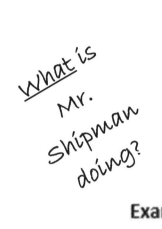

What is Mr. Shipman doing?

Examples use of question words:

Who is the principal of Laster Elementary school?

What does the class do before going to recess?

When does the class go to lunch?

Where is Mr. Shipman's class?

Why is Clifford crying?

How does Mr. Shipman start class every day?

After reading *Mr. Shipman's Kindergarten Chronicles: First Day of School*, answer the following question and color the picture.

Whose leg is Banicia holding?

a) Mrs. Andrews'
b) Mrs. Battle's
c) Mom's

After reading _Mr. Shipman's Kindergarten Chronicles: First Day of School_, answer the following question and color the picture.

Who are the people peeking into Mr. Shipman's classroom?

    a) The other teachers
    b) The parents
    c) The other students

After reading *Mr. Shipman's Kindergarten Chronicles: First Day of School*, answer the following question and color the picture.

Who gives Shuree and Banicia paper and crayons?

  a) Mrs. Laster
  b) Mrs. Green
  c) Mrs. Andrews

After reading _Mr. Shipman's Kindergarten Chronicles: First Day of School_, answer the following question and color the picture.

What is the name of the student who cries for his mother?

a) Clifford
b) JaMarcus
c) Dewayne

After reading *Mr. Shipman's Kindergarten Chronicles: First Day of School*, answer the following question and color the picture.

Which items were colored brown?

a) The girl and the boy
b) The doughnuts and the picture the girl drew of herself
c) The boy's hair

After reading *Mr. Shipman's Kindergarten Chronicles: First Day of School*, answer the following question and color the picture.

What is the name of the activity the students in the picture are doing?

    a) Quiet time
    b) Circle time
    c) Question time

After reading _Mr. Shipman's Kindergarten Chronicles: First Day of School_, answer the following question and color the picture.

According to the story, where is the pirate ship located?

a) In the hallway
b) In the classroom
c) In the library

After reading _Mr. Shipman's Kindergarten Chronicles: First Day of School_, answer the following question and color the picture.

What does Coach Benford teach?

    a) Science
    b) Math
    c) P.E.

After reading *Mr. Shipman's Kindergarten Chronicles: First Day of School*, answer the following question and color the picture.

What are Mr. Shipman and the students preparing to do?

a) Go to lunch
b) Go home
c) Go to recess

After reading _Mr. Shipman's Kindergarten Chronicles:_
First Day of School, answer the following question and
color the picture.

Whose hand is Banicia shaking?

a) Mrs. Andrews'
b) Shuree's
c) Mr. Shipman's

After reading *Mr. Shipman's Kindergarten Chronicles: First Day of School*, answer the following question and color the picture.

Who is Banicia pretending to be?

    a) Mr. Shipman
    b) Mr. Benford
    c) Mom

This certificate is awarded to

_____

for the successful completion of

Mr. Shipman's Kindergarten Chronicles

First Day of School

Learning Workbook and Activities

Answers

Nouns page 48

Dog	rocket	sister	school	brother
Mother	home	cat	cow	

Nouns page 49

List one   **leg**
List two   **table**
List three   **mud**
List four tiger

Nouns page 50

1. Dog
2. Boy
3. Cat
4. Bird
5. Mother/girl
6. Whale/ocean
7. Fish/pond
8. Mr. Shipman/teacher
9. Dewayne
10. House

Nouns page 51

1. Animals
2. Colors
3. Books
4. Houses

Nouns page 52

Homes/rockets/roses/dishes/hands

Nouns page 53

1. Plural/ dogs
2. Singular/ cat
3. Plural/ houses
4. Singular/ mom
5. Singular/ Mr. Shipman
6. Singular/ school
7. Plural/ girls
8. Singular/ boy
9. Singular/ stores
10. Singular/ baby

Common Prepositions page 56

1. With
2. Out
3. With
4. From
5. By
6. On
7. in
8. Off
9. Of
10. For

Forming Sentences -- Page 58 -- The girl jumps up.

Forming Sentences -- Page 59 – The kid plays with the ball.

Forming Sentences – Page 60 -- Sentences will vary.

Question Words – page 63 – C

Question Words – page 64 – B

Question Words – page 65 – C

Question Words – page 66 – A

Question Words – page 67 -- B

Question Words – page 68 -- B

Question Words -- page 69 -- B

Question Words – page 70 – C

Question Words – page 71 – C

Question Words – page 72 – C

Question Words – page 73 – A

Made in the USA
Lexington, KY
30 November 2019